ELLIOTT CARTER

RIGMAROLE

for Bass Clarinet and Violoncello

HENDON MUSIC

BOOSEY & HAWKES

NOTE FROM THE COMPOSER

Rigmarole was composed for the cellist Fred Sherry and the bass clarinetist Virgil Blackwell for my 103rd birthday concert on December 8, 2011 in New York City.

– Elliott Carter

HINWEIS DES KOMPONISTEN

Rigmarole wurde für den Cellisten Fred Sherry und den Bass-Klarinettisten Virgil Blackwell anläßlich meines 103. Geburtstagskonzertes am 8. Dezember 2011 in New York City komponiert.

– Elliott Carter

NOTE DU COMPOSITEUR

Rigmarole fut composé à l'intention de Fred Sherry, violoncelle, et de Virgil Blackwell, clarinette basse, à l'occasion du concert donné pour mon 103ème anniversaire, le 8 décembre 2011 à New York City.

– Elliott Carter

Duration: 2 minutes

for Fred and Virgil

RIGMAROLE

For Bass Clarinet and Violoncello

B♭ Bass Clarinet

Elliott Carter
(2011)

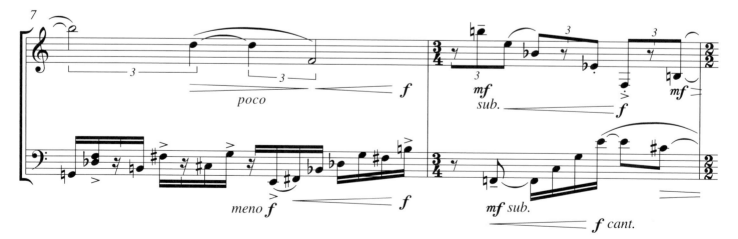

979-0-051-09842-2

Printed in USA
First Printed 2021

ELLIOTT CARTER

RIGMAROLE

for Bass Clarinet and Violoncello

Violoncello Part

HENDON MUSIC

BOOSEY & HAWKES

NOTE FROM THE COMPOSER

Rigmarole was composed for the cellist Fred Sherry and the bass clarinetist Virgil Blackwell for my 103rd birthday concert on December 8, 2011 in New York City.

– Elliott Carter

HINWEIS DES KOMPONISTEN

Rigmarole wurde für den Cellisten Fred Sherry und den Bass-Klarinettisten Virgil Blackwell anläßlich meines 103. Geburtstagskonzertes am 8. Dezember 2011 in New York City komponiert.

– Elliott Carter

NOTE DU COMPOSITEUR

Rigmarole fut composé à l'intention de Fred Sherry, violoncelle, et de Virgil Blackwell, clarinette basse, à l'occasion du concert donné pour mon 103ème anniversaire, le 8 décembre 2011 à New York City.

– Elliott Carter

Duration: 2 minutes

for Fred and Virgil

RIGMAROLE
For Bass Clarinet and Violoncello

Violoncello

Elliott Carter
(2011)

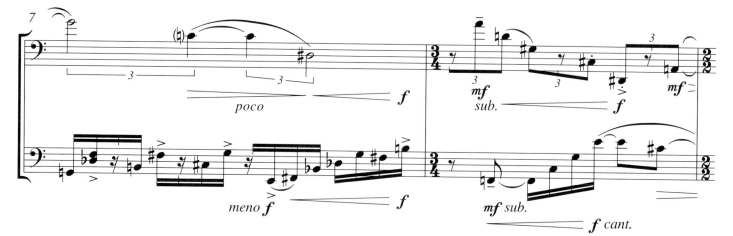

979-0-051-09842-2

Printed in USA
First Printed 2021

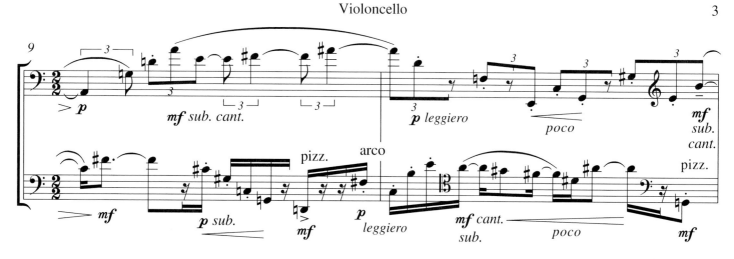

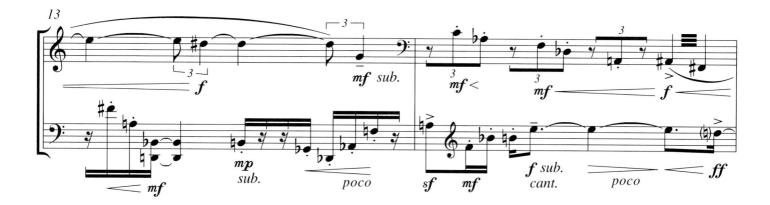

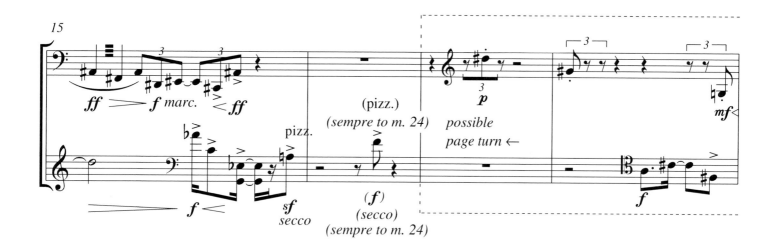

CARTER: *Rigmarole*

If page turn taken on previous page:

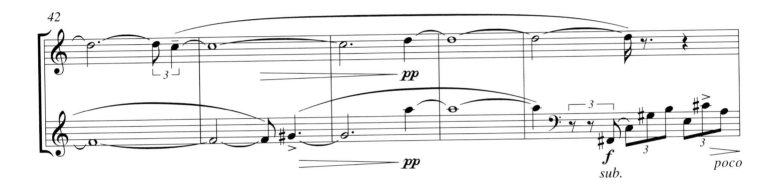

NYC November 5, 2011

CARTER: *Rigmarole*

CARTER: *Rigmarole*

If page turn taken on previous page:

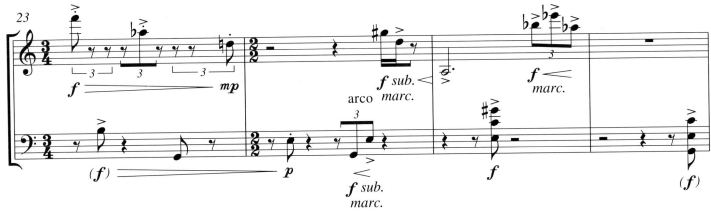

CARTER: *Rigmarole*

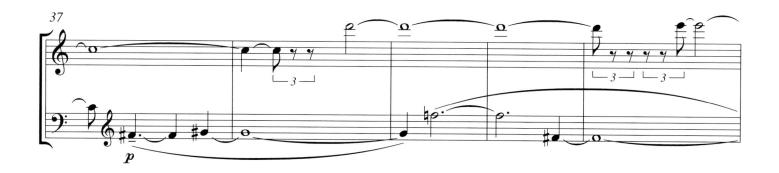

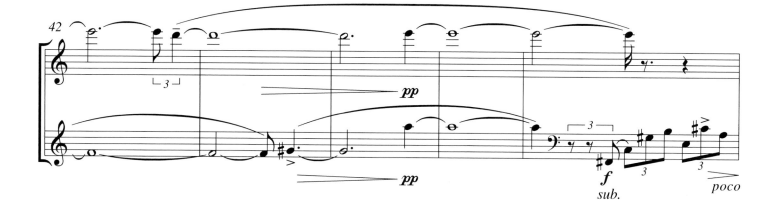

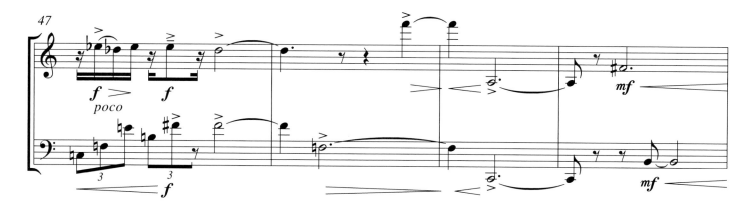

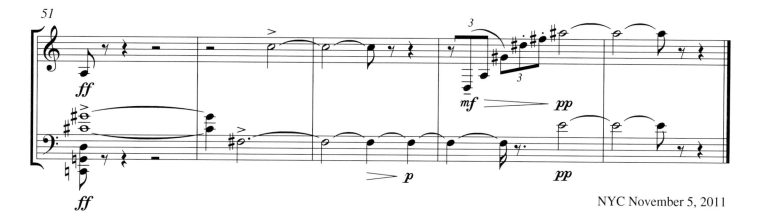

NYC November 5, 2011

CARTER: *Rigmarole*